More Feathers in the Lake than Swans

poems by

Meg Tyler

Finishing Line Press
Georgetown, Kentucky

More Feathers
in the Lake than Swans

Copyright © 2025 by Meg Tyler
ISBN 979-8-88838-979-9 First Edition
All rights reserved under International and Pan-American Copyright Conventions. No part of this book may be reproduced in any manner whatsoever without written permission from the publisher, except in the case of brief quotations embodied in critical articles and reviews.

Publisher: Leah Huete de Maines
Editor: Christen Kincaid
Cover Art: Neta Goren
Author Photo: Marco Bader
Cover Design: Elizabeth Maines McCleavy

Order online: www.finishinglinepress.com
also available on amazon.com

Author inquiries and mail orders:
Finishing Line Press
PO Box 1626
Georgetown, Kentucky 40324
USA

Contents

I.
The Given Life 1
Before Lament 2
Lignum Vitae 3
Trompe l'Oeil 4
Legato 5
Till Ice Becomes Floe 6
An Hour Gained 7
Collecting 8
From the Dock 9

II.
Of Dispositions 13
Cane 14
Red Maples in Winter 15
Beaux Arts 16
Asking and Carrying 17
Mourning 18
Once That Seemed Too Much 19
The Door 20

III.
Impiety 23
Tall Grasses 24
Taken Wing 25
The Landscape Listens 26
Friendly Fire 27
The Good-Bye 28
Almost November 29
Winter in Mt. Auburn Cemetery 30

IV.
Accounts 33
Backfire 34
Little Evil 35
No More Crying 36
The Clearing 37
Ecole Maternelle 38

After Some Years 39
The Spot 40
Emissary 41

V.
The Wake 45
Loosestrife 46
The Heat 47
Second Trimester: Night Sweats 48
Louisa Lake 49
Home 50
After Your Call 51
Lake Maspenock 52
Traffic 53
The Thaw 54
After a Wedding in Richmond, Maine 55

VI.
The Benefits of Misreading: Armor Dresses 59
Of Judgment 60
If This Be Error 61
Autumn Hum 62
To Ireland 63
Returning to Belfast 64
The Art of the Troubles 65
The Geese 66
Turn in the Year 67
In the Top Branches 68
The Glare 69

VII.
Of the Season 73
Mistaken 74
Not Yet 75
Squam Lake, New Hampshire 76
The Words 77
Feathery Layers 78
Of Life 79
The Mud 80
The Notes 81
Of Hands 82

For Marco, Otto and Uriel

One's own reputation—why the fuss?
One's own wealth—why the concern?
I say, what you gain
        is more trouble than what you lose

Love is the fruit of sacrifice
Wealth is the fruit of generosity

Be content,
        rest in your own fullness—
You will not suffer from loss
You'll avoid the snare of this world
You'll have a long life and endless blessings

        Tao Te Ching, Lao Tzu (tr. Jonathan Star)

I.

The Given Life

> *The happiness of any given life is to be measured not by its joys
> and pleasures but by the absence of sorrow and suffering.*
> —Schopenhauer

The forty-minute walk in the deep fresh snow.
We hove into view at the 1/2 mile mark,
red of face, white breath through the cotton
of our masks, like the aftermath of pressing flour.
Our boots weren't tall enough so the snow came in
and cooled our calves. How hard that was
in our layered and mummified outfits. Each step
a conscious and effortful maneuver.
Like the five-minute increments of consciousness
this morning, staring out at the gleam
on snow below the smear of blue sky.
This, then, is my measure. Vagaries of mood,
the pensive clock, more feathers in the lake than swans.

Before Lament

Ceres understood. Transitions were not
to be made alone. She accompanied girls
as they stepped across each threshold:

into the softening approach of womanhood,
the rounding of hip and haunch, the plumping
of breast into a pliable form upon which

a beloved or a child could find solace. She oversaw
each tentative move into married life, giving courage
as she blessed the potential of the framework.

She held each mother's hand and mopped
each clear brow as the sweet small soul came
forward and light through water broke over the world.

Even the dead she cared for, singing softly to them
as they passed into the darkness. In her fields, the earth
displayed its bounty. Grapes glistened in the sun.

Vines strengthened. Wheat made the chaff seem
purposeful. Sunflowers grew taller than the children
who played among them. Was it her fertility that

eventually incurred their wrath? Because
her plough-furrow opened the earth to the realm
of men and created the first field and its boundary?

She brought forth and she sheltered. When she sang,
starlings circled the air, cows looked up with
moonstruck eyes, torches from the *spina alba*

burned brighter. Her justice was in the scent
of the apple's white blossom, the refusal of
the red-flowered hibiscus to feel shame.

Lignum Vitae

From the blue door,
I became aware
of the mouth of the ocean.

Through Caribbean pine,
hibiscus, bougainvillea.
I had woken from a dream

to a dream of the tree of life,
lignum vitae, and a small snake
that spelled its own alphabet
as it curled out of the way.

Wind through the sea grapes.
Cerulean blue, the water. Softer
than it looked with its liquid
shards splintering as it

fizzed onto pink sand. Where
had we gone this time to escape
that which we could not escape.
Connecting the sky to the earth

are the trees' elliptic leaves
above which emerge bluish-purple
flowers in terminal clusters.

Trompe l'Oeil

> *Many go fishing all their lives without knowing
> that it is not fish they are after.*
> —Henry David Thoreau

As when you saw
        a turtle's head break through
the skin of the water
        and first assumed it was
a clump of new oakleaf,

                adrift, after the storm.
                      The mounds of scotch moss
                erupt in pinprick white flowers.
                    A chartreuse pillow,
                tending toward the hyacinth.

Not far away, creeping thyme
        shines emerald, arriving at
its fullest commitment to green.
        Tendril of sweet pea and stem
of woodruff deepen their hues.

                Some greens are sage, yearn blue:
                      the northern pine needles,
                the hostas and lacy artemesia.
                    The hues change with each shift
                of branch, each lash of sunlight.

        By the shore,
the allium leaves, beneath
their ponderous purple globes,
        are dark and thick as knives.

Legato

The snow falling. My fingers stained pink from threading cranberries onto four meters of dental floss. You leaping up from the sofa when you saw through the snow-flecked windowpane the bald eagle land on the ice.

Till Ice Becomes Floe

Before the sun lifts itself up
from the bed of tall pines,
the ice touches the lake
and forms patches of milk-light
around which the mute swans glide.

They will stay here through December,
just until the water stops moving,
solidifies into ice. Feast of milfoil,
curly pondweed. I know
and you know that there are limits

to what we can give. But we keep
going at it, as if people
could be free from that knowledge.
The swans glide, till ice becomes floe,
becomes ripple. At dusk we hear

the flap of their great wings
beating a way out, a way
back, but not and never
beyond.

An Hour Gained

Sunlight, briefly, warms the brisk air.
Oak and maple leaves fall and then flit
above the grass, shifting into a new
arrangement with each gust of wind.
November makes a game of browns
and burnished oranges while whites
and silvers of trunk and limb catch
the last light of day. At night,
the Hunter's Moon through the slit
in the curtains. Separation of the light,
division of bodies.

Collecting

I am sitting in a sunbeam, reading Tagore.
Between trees. The day lilies trumpeting
their something. My shoulders tense
as a dog yips. Heat spreads across
my chest and upper arms. *Where*
our humanity is concerned, we are
very weak—because we do not consider
some human beings as part of mankind.
A bee nuzzles the peony the color
of cotton before it is spun. Boston Ivy
covers the window frames, the ledge stone,
and now the gutter. It patterns the window
glass with its large green hands.
Since we understand difference more
than unity, we will never rid ourselves
of slavery and piteous humiliation.
On the heart-shaped moonflower leaf,
a small dark crawling thing,
a giver and a taker of life,
which the light without effort
collects.

.

From The Dock

> *The mind that is not baffled is not employed.*
> —Wendell Berry

Two figures in a kayak with a blue skin.
One large, one small. Both silent.
The larger one's shoulders move up

and then down with each graceful swipe
of the yellow paddle. He writes a letter
to the lake in the cursive of his movements.

The small one in front as still as a royal
in a carriage. Movement, stillness,
the sleek cut through the waves

the boat makes. Lakeside, delicate flavors
noose the air. Dragonflies glitter. Patterns of sun

and shadow flit across my legs
dangling above the water. The kingfisher,
majestic and intent, takes his dive.

II.

Of Dispositions

> *James Patterson identifies cancers in the nineteenth-century imagination as 'uninvited beasts which surreptitiously ganged up on the body.'* James T. Patterson, The Dread Disease: Cancer and Modern American Culture *(Cambridge, MA: Harvard University Press, 1987),*

From the Greek, *kakos* (of a bad nature,
which you were not) and *hexis* (way of being)
comes *cachexia*, meaning "poor physical state"
which hardly describes your steady wasting.
Bedside, I clasped radius and ulna
and little more. It was your lifelong nature,

like a bird's or a pollen-seeking bee,
to take only what you needed. Cups of tea,
sourdough bread, quiet hours between
the school bus and errands. Sliding
a postcard between the pages of Proust
as you looked out the window

at St. John the Divine. The cancer,
of a bad nature, interacted with
your good. Rapacious, it would have
none of your modesty. From the Latin,
commiseratus, I was *miser*
(wretched), *com* (with).

Cane

> *Our sense of ourselves then becomes a deserted field*
> *at nightfall, with sad reeds flanking a boatless river, bright in the*
> *darkness growing between the distant shores.*
> —Fernando Pessoa, *The Book of Disquiet*

Before bluegrass, river cane covered Kentucky.
                The bamboo shot to thirty feet, rinsing
     the air. Dense thickets, canebrakes, a hide-out
for birds like the passenger pigeon.
                Out of the culms, the Natives made
     baskets and blowguns, tobacco pipes and fish spears.
Then settlers came, the ox and plow, and thousands
            of acres of rivercane, *Arundinaria gigantea*, disappeared.

I think of this, and more, when I see
                the cannula attached to a port near
     your collarbone. Another plastic reed
feeds into your stomach. Remember when
                we drove six hours one springtime,
     to pick up the poet, and swept past riverbanks,
wild rye, and running buffalo clover in your blue Camry?
                Sat with him at the hotel bar, his eyes
     moving up and down to follow a basketball
                on the screen. His whiskey,
     our water, the collective and collecting
straws.

Red Maples in Winter

The lichen makes them look like
birches from a distance, the sun full on,
both the brown-purple reeds and the trees
lit up with the solstice blaze,
made cleaner by the deep snow at their feet.
The first winter when I have not felt
hoodwinked or woebegone or any
of the worry words: *wail, whine,
wane, wobble, want.*

Foliose lichen flower, like chipped
pool paint. The tree trunks, our
sisters, as we walk through leafless
woods and meadow and talk of what
grips us, mothers of children we can
never fully secure. Love keeps them
little, which is why you stare at the
ceiling above the wooden bedframe
that holds you captive each night
when the light has long given out.

Beaux Arts

> *Human life is everywhere a state in which much is to be endured, and little to be enjoyed*
> Samuel Johnson, *Rasselas*

It is over now. The fight. Think

of all the companionable souls

that have made their way through,

out, down or up. Some of us fall,

Icarus-like, while others face

into knowledge elsewhere,

at the edge of a poem about

a stubby field, a pebbled road

running alongside a ditch.

Blackbirds above, on a wire.

Ah!, you'd offer, there were

cicadas for evensong,

Asking and Carrying

When I asked my mother why
she stayed awake all night each
time I flew across the ocean,
she said she was keeping
the plane aloft with her
thoughts. Strange, how two
weeks after you died, my
beautiful friend, I felt as if
I had lost 100 pounds. Had I
been carrying you that long
and that far? Each pound
the cancer took from you,
grief hefted. I thought of this
after the evening thunderstorm
and the drenched heads of
peonies dipped into the grass.

Mourning

> *"It's when we're busy, distracted, sought out, exteriorized, that we suffer most. Inwardness, calm, solitude make us less miserable."*
> Roland Barthes, *Mourning Diary*

To be quiet in myself and left

untroubled by the pertinacious world.

My quest for an hour. Phone rings.

Credit fraud. So. Six varieties

of daffodil open shy faces to the sun.

Last night, rabbits ate the heads

of the red tulips, a few shorn petals

on the ground. Neighbor responds to April

with a leaf blower, drowning out the birds.

Once That Seemed Too Much

Without fuss, the forsythia presents
        its little yellow flags. Closer to ground,
the sprays of hyacinth, Easter-colors,

the day almost silent with few bird songs.
        Tall daffodil, trembling with the first touches
of the bee. I am glad of the return,

these familiars. How they sway gently in the wind,
        nodding to the season. The year of contagion
and boredom behind us. Will we speak closely

to each other's faces again, marvel at the curve
        of a cheek, smoothness of a lip? Mouthing the fibers
of a surgical mask, we incant:

> *Love at the lips was touch*
> *As sweet as I could bear;*
> *And once that seemed too much;*
> *I lived on air*

The Door
for Saskia

The soft almost-golden August fields
near Rheinsberg made want to weep.
Me too, you texted,
from thousands of miles away.
Cornflower, Queen Anne's lace.
Beech and birch and fir trees.
Purple clover, wild morning glory.
All these, ending, you loved
even more. From my side
of the ocean, I imagined you walking
down the marbled stairs to the foyer
with its checkered floor and out the door
to await the little yellow school van.
When I last accompanied you
down those steps, to greet
your dazzling boy, I opened
the iron and glass door
with one hand, embarrassed
by my strength, as you
passed through.

III.

Impiety

After many quiet days, he decided—
as simply as turning down

the covers for the night—to let go
his body forever, so that she

would know that, too:
an awakening, the rose crossing over
to thorn.

Tall Grasses

From a distance, the Downlands mislead.
There, in tall grasses, you lose your bearings.
The names shift. *Bostal. Cuckmere. Field of rape.*

What I grew up calling: path, stream, wildflowers.
Something was at work in me then, loosening,
not proclaimed. That was before you took me

to the thick of it, taught me that if a hawthorn
isn't nipped by a sheep's incisors at two inches
it will burgeon into bush, then carpet scrub.

Taken Wing

The wind catches hard around the corner.
    It shakes the passersby as if they were heavy rugs.
        Past the gas station where the attendant rocks
            in his chair, in his ribs born out of blue stones.
                You, perfect, dead and forever twenty-four.
            In your borderless heaven, there is no winter.
        At the last, did you make a sound? Was it only wind
    that pushed you off, that darkened the pavement,
trickled in crevices, sweet and salty for the ants?

The Landscape Listens

Through the window of the blue
adjoining room—
the moon like the eye
of a netted fish.

He grew shy of his life.

In her hunched the anther of their child,
still dreamless. A surge of cicadas.

Though he took his life, she slept on, wreathing
the net, and woke to cawing and the familiar
play of light across the wall.

Friendly Fire

Ice reaches down from the gutters like old rasta hair.
I perch by the window. Each car that passes, passes.

There is little wonder in this expectancy.
More intent on who does not visit than on who will.

Next to the window, my potted palms stoop like Lowell's Union
Soldiers, home from what they thought would be

a certain death. If someone would just stay put. Only
then I would be safe to know what has grown so sick in me.

The Good-Bye

What made me feel most powerless

was the way your death fell in line
with the season, as if you were only

an individual leaf turning, mostly

imperceptible, mostly wind. Afterwards
they told me to light a candle for you,

to help your spirit leave this earth.

I remember watching the flame swell
and then blowing it out, wanting you

to remain in the scorched in-between

where you had left me. All I could feel
of the child was the sickness

that turned in my stomach, the bile.

Almost November

Morning light flattens the lake.
Each caw distinct. A leaf twirls down,
as slowly as the word that finally makes
its way out of her mouth. Past the ribs
of the elm's empty branches.
The earth is deliberate. Preparing the ground
for frost and then the abominable snow.
An acorn skids down the roof and thuds onto
a stone plastered in wet gold and red leaves.
October is ancient, and like the ancient,
it tears with its unforgiveable history
at the present; let me in.

Winter in Mt. Auburn Cemetery

The linen-colored light spreads through the great
mortified fingers of the European Beech.
When what has been given away does not return,

light reflects from the gravestones, as if they were stars.
Think of all the people this landscape has taken
into its mouth and held like wafers of dust.

And yet it aches with want. Like people gone blind.
But in this pain there is silence, occasional
flutter of blackbirds, the sky an exacting shell of blue.

IV.

Accounts

Leaving the two-year old in the truck she takes
a hoe out of the back to hack at the two
copperheads mating on the gravel.

No sense in being frightened off. Got to attend
to what is there. Later at the table when she told him,
Luther's mouth creased into a smile, reminding

her of the ends of the snake halves twisting on the drive.

Backfire

Luther bent over the dead dog. Shook his head
and whistled. Kicked him to the creek.

Knew Ethel would blow her lid. Cooped up all day
with the whinny of what she hadn't known:

a jet spray faucet; something loose and cool
to wear with the blue dress. Once the dog had slipped

on the rocks and torn his paw. She wasn't there
but said she felt it all the same. Damn dog loved her,

followed her around like meat on a stick. As her mother
reminded her, she had been promised finer things.

Little Evil

Hummingbirds there were the least
of your problems. Went to live there

for the quiet. Found gravel,
a hound's invisible bark. Redbreast,

mockingbird, magpie. Even the gnats
sang. The pine thick with them.

What a wretch you had become,
slack as a city postman's empty sack.

And then the dark things down the hill
that Luther told you to mind out for.

Never know what comes up at night
and how. His twin brother gone

hunting and gone for good.
The Bible tells you so, that greed

will take you. Love the little ones,
breathing in their moth-like cots.

No More Crying

Luther's still there. He likes
the smell of black
powder on his fingers.
The soft swish of pouring it
into the paper cartridge.
Why have a gun
if it don't smoke.

The porch is a rocking spot
where he lingers to hear
the rush of cicadas
come and go, remembering
the doe's fading heartbeat.
The eyes finally fixed
in a glassy stare. That's all
there is to it, he thinks.
Eyes wide-open.
No more crying about it.

The Clearing

Cardinals and rabbits fraught with January daylight.
Inside, more medication and the desultory tick

of the clock. She stops cleaning. The baby's clothes
folded evenly in the dresser, toys arranged
in the baskets like plastic fruit. And the stillness

of Risperedone—slowing to remind her
of his epochal decision not to live. When she did,

dislocated and severe as hail. Where did she put her gloves?
House too straight to find anything, anything.
What it had been like for him, the afterwards. A border

like any other. Papers to pass, imaginable vistas,
taking account. Sky as blue as the madhatter's broth.
The dolls asleep on the sofa, face down.

Ecole Maternelle

Reading Simone Weil and feeling dangerously heightened
I wait for my child in the dreary, stone courtyard of Sainte Marie.

The beautiful French mothers make me think first of the way Weil
starved herself, then of the silky and pliant irides that now hem

the garden. I am as familiar with the barrier that exists
between me and them as I am with the shape of the fingers

that hold my book. *Affliction is a marvel of divine technique.*
None of the mothers smiles back at my dim-bulb smile.

Like a butterfly pinned alive into an album, she writes,
we always want to love. A bell rings and the children bang

open the doors, chattering, released from good behavior.
My straggly-haired daughter's eyes bright with the fear

that I won't be there (I am always there). I ask her what
she did today. "I played with yucky stuff." What? I ask again.

She answers the same. I begin to press through the impeccably-
dressed children and their mothers to speak in my splintered French

to Madame Bresson. Then I hear my girl call to a passing playmate,
"Au revoir, Yucky Stuff!" It is only necessary to know that love

*is a direction not a state of the soul. If one is unaware of this,
one falls into despair at the first onslaught of affliction.* I look up

and smile into the unsmiling eyes of the mother of Jean-Christophe.

After Some Years

A friend reminds me of the wisdom of Buddha:
The comparing mind is the miserable mind.

On the one hand, yes. But on the other.
How I have searched for an image equal
to what you have done or even what you were.

It does not matter which. And if I were
to arrive at one that clicked, that made a sound rise
in my throat like an *Ah* or an *Oh,* like the sudden

strips of color in the azalea out front,
would loss no longer be a loss, but a find.

The Spot

The pavement is clean now. Next to it, the angels
needle the small strip of grass with tapered fingers.

Like grief and doctors, they are not particular
and lose interest easily. Here, you emptied yourself

obscenely, like a can of oil. Sometimes I forget.
But your girl. I read to her at twilight, her room full

of the smell of rice milk. As she sleeps, the shades thin
to eggshell skin. Does she spot the dead beneath

the streetlights, as they go by in their gray shifts?

Emissary
    for Uriel Adriana Saskia

When you ask me why your father died
what can I tell you? He consigned himself

to flying. There was nothing in the sky
that week to warn me. The traffic did not change

direction. No goslings on the river's bank.
What can I tell you but how he filled my eyes

with knapweed. How pregnancy estranged me.
A fish in a paddock. A magnolia growing inside a cat.

A time of shakedown and dream-fabric.
What had been real to me had changed.

When you will ask why, ask steadily.
I am not prepared for this.

I held the breath you were born into.
I armor this field of your cotton.

When you rise in the morning I am there,
in love but not immaculately sent.

He sat up all night long on a Boston rooftop,
the lights of the Citgo sign above the Square

lengthening and then retreating beneath him.
The moon was full. The police reported that

at dawn a woman, leaving for work, glanced out
her window for the weather, saw him falling.

V.

The Wake
    for Marco

Into the lake you go
        and on your left
the loosestrife glow,
        on your right
fledgling grapes hang down
        on vines that twist and choke

around the branches of the oak.
        The wind makes sound
through leaves and stems
        and when you start to swim

above the turtles in their beds below
        an upside down "V" trails your stroke.
Widening and shimmering,
        the wake alone I see

when you have gone behind the tree
        and suddenly afloat I feel
in garden bright with grasses still,
        waiting to see the "V" turn round,

right side up not upside down,
        back to me, bare of foot
and feet on ground.

Loosestrife

> *A photograph's punctum is that accident which pricks me...*
> Roland Barthes, *Camera Lucida*

Lythrum salicaria, its purples marshalled,
edges the lake. Here, in the afternoon glare,
its small clusters lose distinction.

In the photo of you and Uri, from August
four years ago, you loll in the shallows;
lavender and green stripes herald your torsos.

That was when we were still just three.
Uri has her arms around your waist.
You are both looking up at me

as I squint into the lens.
Your eyes are clear and blue,
hers bright and brown.

We are away from the russet warmth
of the house. The photo has no sound
but I can hear the water lapping

the lakeshore and the shrill cry
of the bluejays' chase. The allure
of the images has less to do with

what I see than with what I could lose.
The neighbors thinks of this
as an invasive weed. I dare not pull

a tendril. Then, from the kitchen,
snapping peas and shucking corn,
your voices, amber and honey.

The Heat

Thrum of wing against the window pane.
Ruby-throated hummingbird come

to sip more and yet more sugar water.
Then the drone of an as yet distant

jet ski. The lake is like an anvil
and I think of you pounding

the tomato stakes with tree stumps.
In the warm water, there is little relief.

I move around the pine table,
fingering its knots, small cool caves

that harbor a past without memory.
When the heat is here, I believe

in nothing else. Just as when it snows,
covering the hard brown earth.

Second Trimester: Night Sweats

Little flower, it is not you I am afraid of.
You, under the surface, are what you are.

September morning and the lake mists, is
the color of milk. The surface is still;
below, unseen shadows flit, weeds sway,
small creatures on the lake bed stir the sand

and muck. But I cannot name what it is
I don't see at night. I wake to a sudden terror,
sweat-moist. Our hearts beating like mad.
And the air in the room seems smaller
than the chance of pardon, of reprieve.

Louisa Lake

Two mute swans on Louisa Lake. Throughout April one sat firm and upright in the nest, set on a hump of rock and grass in the middle of the lake, away from trespassing weasels.

The male circled the nest and lake, barking at interlopers: Canadian geese, mallard ducks, even a silent and still (still as an effigy) great blue heron.

Bullfrogs croaked. Turtles sunned on rocks. I pushed the stroller along the path, sweat streaming down my back, the baby boy asleep and then smiling. I pushed the stroller through that month and the next, awaiting the arrival.

Meanwhile the heat set in and the lake grew swampy, full of lily pads and millweed and surface growths. Rarely did a current ripple the water. The swans no longer looked sleek and white but as dishwater-colored as the lake. I saw the swans swimming sometimes near the nest, picking at the weed. I felt a loss in my center; I knew it, the babies were dead, maybe stillborn, or carried off and eaten by an intruder.

Now when I saw the swans from a distance their heads dipped down as they searched listlessly for weed. I told my husband what had happened, how it made my core ache. To have waited so long, and for nothing.

We walked together on the weekend, taking turns pushing the stroller. He pointed to the lake. And through the tangled green growth we saw the pair of white swans followed by two dishwater-colored babies, camouflaged by the murky water and weeds.

Home

When I cleared the hill of brush and laid down stones,
onto which you were supposed to pour pebbles

for a drive, my desire was to make—no matter
the steepness of descent—a straighter path to the door.

We got distracted. The pebbles never happened,
although I recall them now as the lentils fall into the pot.

We kept the stairs that wind up and through
the greenery and when you leave the car,

still breathing its hot city breath,
you step down into the walkway made of timber,

surrounded by forsythia, holly and giant fern.
The coolness is a surprise and a relief. Not like

inside after I open the refrigerator door, the house
thick with humidity, and think of the electricity bill.

After Your Call

The branches of the white birch grow bare, nearly ossified.
Creasing the bark are dark tattoos, bold strokes against a landscape
that slowly mutes its color before deciding on a few livid shades.

Lake Maspenock

The snow covers everything: lake, branches,
rooftops, the planks on the dock, even the tip-top

of the weathervane. As if playing a game,
I take giant steps through the feet of snow

to reach the frozen shore where the sun
on the ice then blinds me. Whatever the season,

we always head toward the lake.
In summer, it is love for the glittering motion.

In winter, it is defiance against despair.
The cold burns my cheeks and lips.

I feel alone for a moment on a glacier.
But then I sense movement in the black tree

branches: crows. Each time they leap,
then flutter and land, snow pelts the snow.

Like conscience, which cannot stay clear.
Blue winter sky, solitary sun, hieroglyphic of crow.

Traffic

A few patches of snow glitter quietly
in the shade. Sun like a yolk in a sea
of holy blue. The earth, at last less

niggardly in its thaw, begins to give
beneath my feet as I walk the garden's
perimeters, prune-colored juice

sluicing around pebbles and blades
of bleached grass. Finches twitter
as they pass above, like commas broken

loose from the pack, the sole dark flittings
in a sky as clear as sanity, in a sky
that traffics, for today, in pure sound.

The Thaw

Before dawn, the light
is trapped in the ice.
Then the dark masses
on the far side of the lake
start to take form:
hemlock, maple, oak.

We have been lying here all night,
our sleep broken now and then
by the baby, rearing up
like a prairie dog, to say his say.

Dreams cut off, but not cleanly,
like the branches of the dogwood
when the ice dam finally fell.

After a Wedding in Richmond, Maine

On an April morning the snow drifts and settles
like thought. The landscape imagined itself this way.
It put the birch trees here, the forsythia there.
And then it waited to see what would happen.
What the sun and clouds would bring,
fragrant gifts, the simple stillness of winter.
Everywhere these traces configure themselves.
Like the way the patches of daffodils seem to follow
an arbitrary design. And the birds, what meaning
do they have here. Purple finches. Merely a smear
of color around the feeder. Voles waiting
underground. The swirl of a red squirrel's tail
beside the woodpile. What could be more fundamental.

VI.

The Benefits of Misreading: Armor Dresses

(after looking at sculptures of dresses made from steel armor on Center Trail in Hopkinton MA)

The sunlight strikes
the torso of the word
and I see *Amour*
as a noun preceding
the verb.

How does love dress itself,
I wonder. With steel
instead of fabric
gathered at the waist.

These garments keep.
Will endure wind and weather.
Love is not love which alters
when it alteration finds.

When it fits well, love dresses
the wounds it inflicts. Is a suture,
a plaster. Gives off a defiant sheen,
reflecting all it is cast against.

Whatever part of speech
dresses the form,
cinched or not,
love stands armed,
aimed, the ever-fixed mark
even when aflight.

Of Judgment

Mockingbirds, wrens, nuthatches.
The hydrangea outside the window
quivers just so. Last night I heard
and then saw the sudden rapturous
wheeling of broken light over the water.
Fireworks that dazzle July's darkness.
In Whistler's *Nocturne in Black
and Gold, the Falling Rocket,*
the oranges and golds pulse
among the blacks and greys.
The suggestion of ember and fizzle.
Like Ruskin's sneering claim, that
the painter was "flinging a pot of paint
in the public's face." What we think,
what we know.

If This Be Error

Light spills over the furniture.
The salmon-colored sofa, the serpentine
sideboard. Outside, icicles gleam
like mammoth tusks, and drip.

I have inhabited this room,
along with your voice, for much
of the winter. Mornings, afternoon
—you call me away from the soliloquy,

where the lines I speak hardly change.
Like the drifts of snow and
the radial black branches of the cherry.
I recall our first night. The trees

were in leaf. Words glistened
between us like new stars,
the syllables punctuating the night air.
I saw a slight tremor above your right eye.

And the boyish blush in your cheek.
The moon kept rising. We walked along
the shore of a black lake. As if on cue,
the ineluctable good-bye.

Our awkwardness. You bowed, slightly.
Then you were gone. Leaving me
to work out the transfer of language by myself,
the bed galactic, the earth now turning

the other way.

Autumn Hum

> *Bronze by gold heard the hoofirons, steelyringing.*
> *Imperthnthn thnthnthn.*
>   James Joyce, Sirens, *Ulysses*

The scent ferment

now spikes the air.
Sizzle of cricket.

Maple begins to blush.
October lights the way.

Flickersome, oaksome.
Dash of chip-

munk, scutters, leaf fall.
Some tweet. Lily pads

overbrim the pond,
mostly muck now.

A space has opened
inside me—like music

parting the air. But a silence

with statues. A dignity.
Not like the what next,

the winter to come.

To Ireland

Wherever you look, here
on your green island—hedge,
tarmac, roof tile, red post box—
in all the steadfast markers
of your land there is a glistening
and soon to be another shift
in the wind beneath
the lowering sky.

Can you know what
it means to live in a land
where dryness cracks the earth,
where even ivy turns brown
from the heat, where summer beats
the anvil that the earth
has become?

Returning to Belfast

Two blackbirds cross the motorway to the east.
Gorse like saffron, patching up the side of the hill.

Darkest green clusters are of heather, sedge.
Brown stains where the water won't catch.

Tall pines crest above the billowing oaks.
White of farmhouses. A paddock of white cows.

Who climbs these hills? Dog or man? The day paints itself
green and gray with soft sweep of lavender.

Divis and Black Mountain ahead. From Dark Pool
to Dark Back. Names with an eye to the weather.

The Art of the Troubles
  The Ulster Museum, Belfast, 2014

    The first thing I saw
        was a woman blown high
            by a blast. An iron cast.
Then, to the left, an open

    mouth, the colors smeared,
        the no sound that came out,
            receding but registered by
Le Brocquy, whose brush

    insists on features
        that peel away
            to another shore of
being. In the next room,

    an abandoned island,
        segmented by crumbling
            stone walls. Gerard Dillon's house.
Three donkeys, painted sheep.

    The waves blue and quiet,
        not crashing, the only
            sound from an outboard motor
of the two men on their way.

The Geese
> *As wild geese that the creeping fowler eye,*
> *Or russet-pated choughs many in sort, Rising and cawing at the gun's report,*
> *Sever themselves and madly sweep the sky*
>   *Midsummer Night's Dream*, III, ii, 15-19

The geese honking became the way the dream ended,
its images flapping off the reel. Danger, I thought,
as they directed the others to fly away from
a pair of swans edging closer.

Soon the geese were in flight,
their cries longer, pulling up my thoughts
hand over hand, like an anchor loosened
from the bed of sleep, letting in the daylight.

I was dreaming of which books
to give you, Jack Gilbert or Frank Bidart,
to kick open the trapdoor.
Suddenly I was aware of sound,

light streaming in, my warm head
sunk on a pillow, before the purchase
had been made or the book
chosen.

Turn in the Year

The earth begins its tribute
to dying. The leaves and
the grasses lighten, like hair.
What doesn't time bleach?
The promise of thrush and starling?

What thawed could now freeze.
The stone steps are covered in a damp mass
of yellow and orange leaves.
Roses shed their petals. The air is cold.
The water is cold. The mud slick banks
of the river are hardening.

In the Top Branches

The ice would not unseize
although the lake beneath it
hissed and popped like a stew

as it fights toward the air. We poked
the ice with sticks until they broke.
Then paddles. Even the earth

would not give way, not to pick
or shovel. The endless winter
kept on. Wrens fluttered in the top

branches of the arborvitae.
We waited. Inside,
I cupped the store-bought lilies'

cool petals in my palm,
the pollen dust as orange as the sun
that set some months ago.

The Glare

> *You lie in our bed as if an orchard were over us.*
> *You are what's fallen from those fatal boughs.*
> *Where will we go when they send us away from here?*
>   David Ferry, "In Eden"

When we loosen ourselves from what fixes us

here, will we find in the shadows a race

of wind or something recognizable, like the

pulses of light through an emerald canopy?

Wherever it is, in that place after we end, I

pray that we leave behind the exposure, the

trees cleared from the shore, the glare.

VII.

Of the Season

The flower farmer tells us that
the frost that might come tonight,
first of the season, will blacken
the petals of the dahlias. Thousands
of them, now in rows in the sunlight,
faces as open as the prayer he makes
to her, above. Each cream-orange
or coral frond stores the long
summer's sweetness in its hues.

Seed your grass before mid-October,
he says, before the temperatures shift
and the light dims. The inner needles
of the thuja yellow while the outer
leaves of maples go fluorescent.
The afternoon sun still strong enough
that I squint when I look back
at its reflection on the lake's surface.
Feel me burn, feel my little fire,
it cries, *I'm not ready to be put out.*

Mistaken

Who are you, waving at me across the car park?
Without hesitation, I wave back even as I see in your eye
the mistake. Our lives thunder past. The times of
stillness too. Catching faces as we glance, it all
dissolves, after a while, in sunlight. Like moments of
giddiness, as when we finished exams and burst
out of the building free.

I fold over the top of the sheet and neatly tuck
in the side, to make the bed seem open
for the next sleeper. I wash the towels,
dry the glasses on the rack. My eyes have swept
these walls, the paintings, the wooden floors
countless times. My thoughts, welcome and
unwelcome visitors. Between the bricks on the
walkway, the plantain leaves have flowered
into green spindles. Threading past are boats,
on parade, leaving behind their seams
of glistening water.

Not Yet

Out of the fog a white swan gliding,
trailing a liquid V. Stretching its neck
as it moves through the lake water.
The trees strain to leaf. Pink cherry blossoms
scattered on the grass. A squat wren
hurls a melody lighter than air from the lilac.
The dogwood awakens. Not yet the lilies,
nor the rhododendron. This is my pace.

Squam Lake, New Hampshire

Water clear to the sandy, boulder-dotted floor.
Pines, hemlocks. The loon parent circles
the nest, its whites and blacks strident
against the blue-green water. Eyes that glow
like charcoal. From the shore I swim out
towards the deeper parts, away from the nest.
The loon dunks its head then rises up,
stretches its neck like a faucet, shakes
something down (a crayfish?).
The quiet, birdsong-specked, like a bath
I've stepped into at end of day.
No human voice. No dread machine.
Rather, as hushed as the movement
of blood through veins. As resplendent.

The Words

Over the phone, the ocean
between us, we don't say them.
But they are still there, falling
like lost stars behind the
desultory back and forth.

Feathery Layers

> *Ages pass, and still thou pourest, and still there is room to fill.*
> Rabindranath Tagore, *Gitanjali*

The summer solstice, I wear settledness
around me like a shawl knit by your mother
in Chennai. Sloping towards the lake,
the garden gives over its colors to summer.

Greens rush toward the water's edge,
then stop. Twitters, buzzing, croaks.
The dogwood leans over to give
your mother its flowers. As you

remind me, what we have already
is enough. Here we can keep
the noise of the artificial world
at bay. Your bright laughter,

the lapping of lake water, the hour's
sweet oblivion, like the peony
whose feathery layers will soon
rest shriveled on the path.

Of Life
    for Otto

The winter came on. Snow swirled; frost patched the glass. To pass time, I ate fuji apples, raspberries and kiwi, shipped from afar. Little shiny segments, red, green and white, in a ceramic bowl. Not as sweet as summer fruit but I still hungered for the juice. Feeding into the growing river of your life.

When I finally held you in the nook of my arm, the scent of some pure source cleared the air. Soon, the days began to offer more light. And out there, in the awakening garden, crocuses, small mouths open to the sun.

The Mud

Lake waters were drawn down eight feet this winter.
What once leaked fractured light all day is now mud slick,
not crystallized by salt or sediment. Its sheen muted
by the cadaverous husks of weeds. Seven swans across
a field of sludge from me. Yesterday the child ran into
the muck, thinking it solid. As light as he was,
he sank two feet. My husband set boards across
the sand onto the wet surface of the brown ooze,
then stepped across and pulled him up,
one leg at a time, minus a blue boot. Cold gray
January day. I stood on the dock, calling out
to both of them, electric razor in my mittened hand.
I had been shearing my husband's hair
when the boy got stuck. A breeze picked up
the soft brown-gray tufts and floated them
down onto the recalcitrant mud.

The Notes

The clematis vines into its top knot
of magentas, each petal's color like cabernet
at the bottom of a swirling glass.

After putting down his bow, the child
strokes the white keys of the piano
as his violin teacher opens the hutch

to feed Attila the Bun. Outside,
the flowers of her mimosa tree brighten
the air like the notes she will teach him

to play: E, F, C sharp. Her gentle alertness
to the boy's shifting gaze and sudden movements
from instrument to instrument is echoed by

the bunny's delicate awareness, registered
in his whiskers, which are as long as his body is wide.
Sympathetic vibrations, she says.

The wordless conversations between them:
A to D string, teacher to child, the sound
waves that keep us tuning and in tune.

Of Hands

June heralds the eruption
of *Hemerocallis*, clematis and astilbe
which spill onto the brick walkway
and brush our ankles as we pass.

You were washing the sailboat
and I was reading *East West Street,*
thinking about Philippe Sands and
his use of the words *recusancy*

and *quiescen*t about what passed
on the streets of Lvov, when suddenly,
fully-clothed you fell off the dock
into the water, a bright splashing

sound and then, your laughter.
The child, with his back to you,
carefully sanding the copper barrel
on his homemade wooden musket,

didn't flinch or lift his eyes
so lost was he in the beautiful
labor of his hands.

Acknowledgments

Grateful acknowledgment is made to the editors of the following journals in which these poems first appeared:

Agni: "The Clearing"
"The Fault in the Rock"
"Friendly Fire"
"Encounter"
Del Sol Review: "Little Evil"
Kenyon Review: "The Goodbye"
"Emissary"
"Impiety"
Literary Imagination: "Almost November"
"Taken Wing"
"Ecole Maternelle"
"Before Lament"
"After a Storm"
Literary Matters: "Turn in the Year"
Poetry Northeast: "Tall Grasses"
"The Dead"
Salamander: "Returning to Belfast"
SpoKe: "The Art of the Troubles"
"The Notes"
Zoland Press Poetry Annual: "Winter in Mt. Auburn Cemetery"

Finishing Line Press published a selection of 28 of these poems in *Poor Earth,* 2013 New Women's Voices Chapbook Series

Meg Tyler teaches Humanities at Boston University where she also directs a poetry series. She was the 2016 Fulbright Professor of Anglophone Irish Writing at Queen's University in Belfast and the Fulbright Visiting Professor of Humanities and Social Sciences at the University of Innsbruck in 2012. Her book on Seamus Heaney, *A Singing Contest*, was published by Routledge in their series, Major Literary Authors. *Poor Earth* was published by Finishing Line Press in their New Women's Voices Chapbook Series in 2013. Her poems and prose have appeared in *Agni, Literary Imagination, Kenyon Review, Harvard Review, Irish Review* and other journals. A recent chapter on Heaney and the Eclogue ("Words that the rest of us can understand") can be found in *Heaney's Mythmaking*, edited by Ian Hickey and Ellen Howley (Routledge, 2023). Her essay on "The Plaints of Robert Lowell," appeared in *Robert Lowell in Context*, edited by Thomas Austenfeld and Grzegorz Kosc (Cambridge University Press, 2024). She lives in Massachusetts with her family.

www.ingramcontent.com/pod-product-compliance
Lightning Source LLC
Chambersburg PA
CBHW030053170426
43197CB00010B/1512